# Contents

# What are spiders?

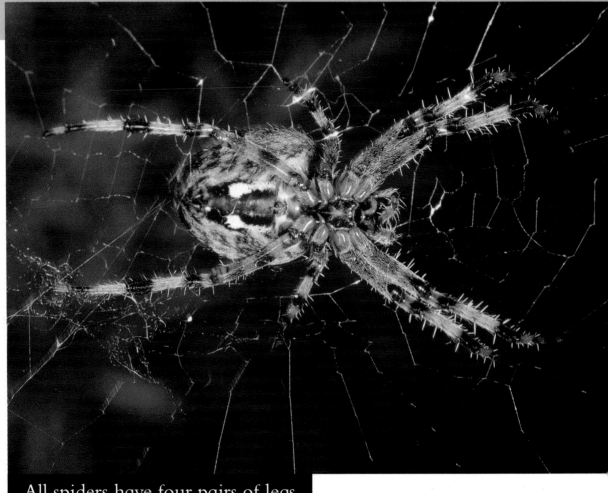

All spiders have four pairs of legs.

Spiders are small animals with eight legs. Spiders cannot fly. All spiders are **predators**. Most spiders spin **webs** to catch their **prey**. **Insects** get stuck in the sticky web and then the spiders eat them.

Some other spiders which live in hot countries are bigger than your hand. Some spiders are so big that they can eat birds and frogs.

Some spiders can be as big as your hand.

# How are spiders born?

The **male** spider taps on the **female's web** so that she will not think that he is an **insect** and kill him. They **mate** and the female spider lays eggs.

The male spider taps on the female's web.

The female black widow spider eats the male after mating!

Female spiders spin a bag to lay their eggs in. This bag is called a **cocoon**. The cocoon is put in a safe place with more web as a lid.

This spider has made a cocoon to keep her eggs safe.

cocoon

# How do spiders grow?

Baby spiders have pale yellow bodies.

Baby spiders are tiny when they first **hatch** out of their eggs. They look like their parents but their bodies are pale yellow. Baby spiders cannot see when they are first born.

The baby spiders grow. They make a new skin and the old skin drops off. This is called **moulting**. Baby spiders moult about five times as they grow.

This baby spider is moulting.

# What do spiders eat?

This spider is waiting for an insect to get stuck in its web.

Spiders eat flies and other **insects** which get stuck in the **web**. The spider knows an insect is stuck when the web moves. The spider poisons the insect with its **fangs**. The poison makes the inside of the insect soft.

The spiders suck the soft parts of the insect up into their mouths. They leave the hard outside part. Some very big spiders eat lizards, birds and frogs.

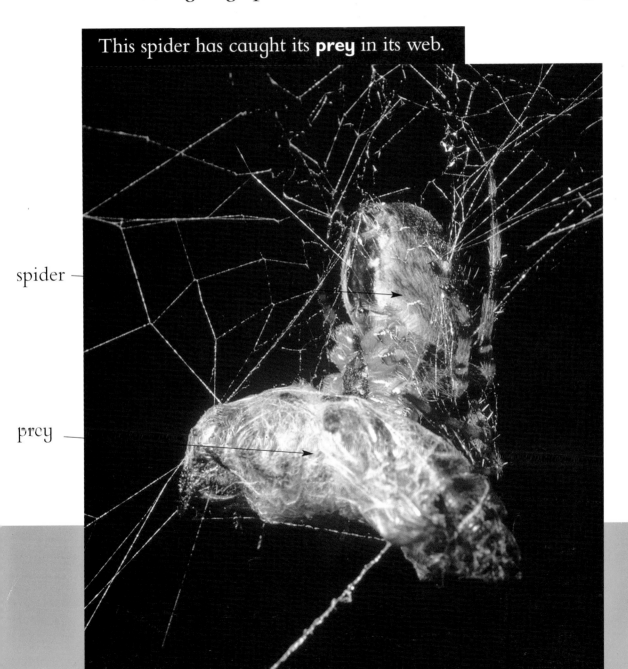

This spider has caught its **prey** in its web.

spider

prey

15

# Which animals attack spiders?

Many animals and **insects** attack spiders. Hunting wasps attack spiders from behind. They jump on them and then carry them back to a tunnel in the ground. The spiders cannot move. Hunting wasps eat spiders alive.

This hunting wasp has caught a spider.

Frogs like to eat spiders.

Birds, ants and frogs attack spiders too. They all like to hunt spiders for food. But the very worst enemies of a spider are other spiders. Many spiders get eaten by other spiders!

# Where do spiders live?

Spiders live in many different places. Spiders live in parks, woods and gardens. They live in houses and sheds. Some live in holes between stones. Other spiders like to live under damp, dark leaves.

A spider has made its home in the branches of this bush.

Spiders live on mountains and in hot deserts.
Many spiders live in dark caves. Some tiny spiders
even live in the fur of big animals!

A trapdoor spider lives in a tunnel in the ground.

# How do spiders move?

Spiders walk on their eight legs.

Spiders use their eight legs to walk. They move their legs two at a time. Some spiders can move as fast as people.

Crab spiders can walk sideways and backwards.

This spider has oily pads on its feet to stop it sticking to the web.

**Insects** get stuck in **webs** very quickly. But a spider has special oily pads on its feet. The oil stops the spider from sticking to the webs.

# How long do spiders live?

Most spiders live for a year.

Most spiders live for about a year but many spiders die when they are babies. Sometimes the **female** spider eats the **male** spider after they have **mated**.

A purse web spider in Britain lived for nine years.

Some big spiders live longer than a year. A tarantula is a big spider that lives in hot countries. This spider can live for twenty years if it is kept as a pet.

This pet tarantula could live for twenty years.

# What do spiders do?

spider's web

This web will have taken about an hour to build.

Spiders make **webs** and look for food. They rest in quiet, dark places. The spider builds its web early in the morning. This takes about an hour.

There are over 40,000 different kinds of spider in the world.

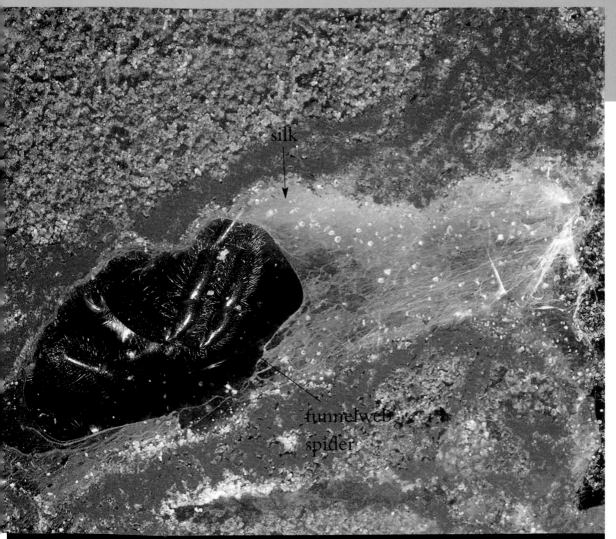

silk

funnelweb spider

The funnelweb spider makes a soft burrow of silk under the ground.

The funnelweb spider lives under the ground.
It makes a **burrow** where it can be cool and
damp. Then it spins silk to make the burrow soft.

The funnelweb spider can be found in
Sydney in Australia.

# How are spiders special?

Spiders are special because they have very sensitive hairs on their legs. The sensitive hairs move if an **insect** lands on the **web**. This tells them that food is coming.

leg hairs

A spider's special leg hairs tell it when an insect is trapped.

Spiders are also special because they can make silk. The silk comes out of **spinnerets** which are like little fingers underneath the spider. The silk is very strong.

The spider produces a liquid from its spinnerets. It turns to silky thread when it touches the air.

silk thread

spider

# Thinking about spiders

Now you have read about spiders can you answer these questions?

1   This spider can change its colour to match the flower it is hiding on. What is this spider called? (See page 7.)

2   What do you think this spider eats?

Why does this spider change colour?

3   How long has it taken the spider to make this web? (See page 24.)
4   How does the web help the spider?

When does a spider make its web?

# Bug map

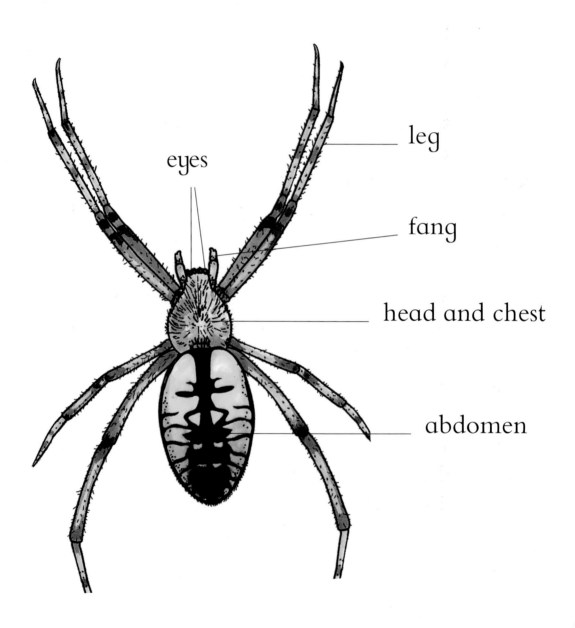

eyes

leg

fang

head and chest

abdomen

# Glossary

**burrow**  a long hole which looks like a tunnel in the ground

**cocoon**  a silk bag which the female makes to hold the eggs

**fangs**  claws on the spider's head which are used to poison insects

**female**  a girl

**hatch**  when a baby animal comes out of its egg

**insect**  a small animal with six legs

**male**  a boy

**mate**  the male and the female join up to make babies

**moulting**  when the spider grows a new skin and the old skin drops off

**predator**  an animal that hunts other animals for food

**prey**  an animal that is hunted by another animal for food

**spinnerets**  are like short fingers under the back of the spider's body. These are used for making silk.

**web**  a pattern made from sticky threads of silk, which the spider uses to catch food

# Index